New Mexico Bucket List Adventure Guide & Journal

Explore The Natural Wonders & Log Your Experience!

Bridge Press

Bridge Press
dp@purplelink.org

Please consider writing a review!
Just visit: purplelink.org/review

ISBN: 978-1-955149-12-9

FREE BONUS

Find Out 31 Incredible Places You Can Visit Next! Just Go To:

purplelink.org/travel

Table of Contents:

How to Use This Book

Welcome to your very own adventure guide to exploring the natural wonders of the state of New Mexico. Not only does this book lay out the most wonderful places to visit and sights to see in the vast state, but it also serves as a journal so you can record your experience.

Adventure Guide
Sorted by region, this guide offers 50 amazing wonders of nature found in New Mexico for you to go see and explore. These can be visited in any order, and this book will help keep track of where you've been and where to look forward to going next.

Each portion describes the area or place, what to look for, how to get there, and what you may need to bring along. A map is also included so you can map out your destinations.

Journal Your Experience
Following each location description is a fillable journal page for you. During or after your visit, you can jot down in the journal portion significant sights encountered, events confronted, people involved, and memories you gained while on your adventure. This will add even more value to your experience and keep a record of your time spent witnessing the greatest wonders of New Mexico.

GPS Coordinates and Codes
As you can imagine, not all of the locations in this book have a physical address. Fortunately, some of our listed wonders are either located within a national park or reserve or are near a city, town, or place of business. For those that are not associated with a specific location, it is easiest to map it using GPS coordinates.

Luckily, Google has a system of codes that converts the coordinates into pin-drop locations that Google Maps is able to interpret and navigate.
Each adventure in this guide will include the GPS coordinates along with general directions on how to find the location and Google Plus codes whenever possible.

How to find a location using Google Plus:

1. Open Google Maps on your device.
2. In the search bar, type the Google Plus code as it is printed on the page.
3. Once the pin is located, you can tap on "Directions" for step-by-step navigation.

It is important that you are prepared for poor cell signals. It is recommended to route your location and ensure that the directions are accessible offline. Depending on your device and the distance of some locations, you may need to travel with a backup battery source.

About New Mexico

Originally colonized by Spain, New Mexico became a United States territory in 1853 as part of the Gadsden Purchase. Even though the land of New Mexico was considered part of the US, it officially became the 47th state in 1912. Home to over two million people, New Mexico, sits in the south of the United States. Because of its lush landscape and culture, New Mexico has been nicknamed the Land of Enrichment. But aside from its beautiful landscape, rich culture, and endless attractions, New Mexico has a unique history.

During World War II, the Manhattan Project began its nuclear research on New Mexico's soil. Scientists worked in New Mexico as they raced to create the world's most powerful—and devastating— bomb. On July 16, 1945, the first atomic bomb was tested at the Trinity bomb site near the city of Alamagordo. It is said that people who lived over 150 miles from the test site could still feel the impact of the explosion.

New Mexico has also had mysterious encounters with possible extraterrestrial life. In 1947, a local farmer from Roswell, New Mexico, found unusual debris on his property and claimed it was the remains of an alien spaceship. While the US Air Force claimed it was simply a crashed air balloon, others knew that it was virtually impossible for a human to survive that high of a crash and even used test dummy experiments to prove it. Since then, the town of Roswell has become a popular destination for those interested in extraterrestrial life.

Because of its endless options for tourism and activities, New Mexico is a prime destination for road trippers, families, and adventurers alike. Outdoor enthusiasts can explore New Mexico's numerous national forests and parks, ski at its eight ski resorts, go white water rafting, and camp in the backcountry wilderness. At night, the stars fill the sky in a way that cannot be found in major cities. For the ultimate sky gazing experience, visit one of New Mexico's Dark Sky Parks.

For those interested in New Mexico's unique history, New Mexico has several Native American museums that promote the art, pueblos, and culture of these sovereign nations. New Mexico is well known for its art communities, and visitors can visit its many art museums and attractions. Not only can visitors interact with the artists who are inspired by New Mexico's culture and landscape, but they can visit the home of Georgia O'Keeffe, an artist who was enamored with New Mexico and moved to the state's capital of Santa Fe to be closer to the landscape.

If tourists are interested in a spooky historical experience, a visit to one of New Mexico's 400 ghost towns is a must. Most of these towns sprang up during the rush for mining gold, silver, copper, lead, coal, and turquoise but were suddenly abandoned, and their populations vanished. To see bits of history, remnants of towns, and old mining equipment, visitors should explore New Mexico's ghost towns.

Landscape and Climate

New Mexico spans 121,590 square miles and is the fifth-largest state in the United States. It is composed of six separate regions: Northwest, North Central, Northeast, Central, Southwest, and Southeast. New Mexico is situated in the southernmost part of the United States and shares borders with Arizona on the west and Texas to the east. Additionally, New Mexico shares its border with Mexico.

New Mexico offers a diverse landscape that includes heavily forested mountains and vast arid deserts. With three distinct topographic regions, New Mexico has a varied landscape that any visitor can appreciate. The Rocky Mountain zone spans across the north-central part of New Mexico and offers gorgeous mountain views, and may be one of New Mexico's most stunning characteristics. There are 23 mountain ranges in total, such as San Juan and Sacramento. The plains region covers most of New Mexico and extends from the eastern border to the Sangre de Cristos and the Guadalupe mountain ranges. The Great Plains cover about one-third of New Mexico's landscape and are characterized by large flatlands that have few trees and little change in elevation.

In addition to the plains and mountains, the third topographic region of New Mexico is the intermountain plateau, which is an elevated area that is generally found between mountains.
The elevation ranges from 2,817 feet at Red Bluff Lake to New Mexico's highest peak, Wheeler Peak, which is 13,161 feet in elevation. Elephant Butte Lake is New Mexico's largest lake at nearly 40 miles long and includes more than 200 miles of shoreline.

New Mexico's climate is dry and does not experience extreme weather conditions. When it comes to sunshine, New Mexico is one of the sunniest states in the US. In fact, New Mexico comes in second place behind Arizona for most days of sunshine each year.

Because of its elevation, New Mexico does have four seasons. Generally, the weather will have hot days that cool off overnight. During the summer, the occasional scattered thunderstorm is to be expected. In the winter, the weather will stay moderate, and some areas will get heavy snow. While spring and fall feature some of the most gorgeous weather (65 to 85°F), spring is known for being more unpredictable for temperatures and weather.

While the highest temperature recorded in New Mexico was 122°F, the average temperature in the summer is around 97°F. However, it's not uncommon for hot summer days to consistently exceed 100°F. In the winter, the temperature will drop below freezing (less than 0°F) in many places. In fact, the record coldest temperature ever recorded in New Mexico was -50°F. However, the winter temperatures are milder in lower elevations.

The temperatures will vary greatly from day to night because of the effect of the sun and low humidity. Additionally, altitude also plays a major role in the temperature. While the higher altitudes may have cooler temperatures, the lower altitudes may feature warmer to more moderate temperatures.

Map of New Mexico

White Sand National Monument

Because of its vast white sand dunes, this park is breathtaking. At the center of the Tularosa Basin, White Sand is the largest gypsum sand dune field. Gypsum sand is rare because this sand easily dissolves when it comes into contact with water, making this spot truly unique.

Best time to visit:
White Sand National Monument is open every day of the year except December 25th. The weather will be warm year-round, but the best time to visit White Sand for mild temperatures is in October/November.

Pass/Permit/Fees:
White Sand charges a $25 fee per vehicle upon entering the park, but if there is only one person in the car, the fee is only $15. There are options for annual passes.

Closest city or town: Holloman Air Force Base and Alamogordo, NM

How to get there:
One way to get to the park is to enter "white sands" into a GPS, but sometimes GPS will take you 25 miles west of the park to White Sands Missile Range. The visitor's center can be found on Dunes Drive and is located just off Highway US-70. The entrance is between the cities of Alamogordo and Las Cruces, and the turn to get into the park is between mile markers 199 and 200 on US-70. Also, there are no gas stations in the park, so visitors are encouraged to fill their tanks in Alamogordo before coming to White Sand.

GPS Coordinates: 32° 46' 45" N, 106° 10' 19" W

Did You Know?

In 1933, White Sand was declared a national monument. But in 2019, it was renamed a national park. The park itself is situated between several military bases, which sometimes causes it to be closed due to missile tests. So, before making the journey to White Sand, visitors should always check online for park closures.

Journal:

Date(s) Visited:

Weather conditions:

Who you were with:

Nature observations:

Special memories:

Carlsbad Caverns

Carlsbad Caverns is the main attraction of Carlsbad Caverns National Park. Nestled in the Guadalupe Mountains of New Mexico, this spot is full of rocky slopes, deep canyons, and underground caves that are waiting to be explored.

Best time to visit:
Carlsbad Caverns has warm weather year-round and almost always has sunshine. However, the best time to visit is in the fall (October/November).

Pass/Permit/Fees:
Permits to hike and camp in the backcountry are free, but visitors should get their permits ahead of time. Research, events, and cave exploration require a permit.

Closest city or town: White City, NM

How to get there:
The best way to get to the park is to enter the address for their visitor's center: 727 Carlsbad Caverns Highway. Once you turn off the only entrance from Carlsbad Caverns Highway, you'll encounter 11 miles of scenic roads before arriving at the visitor's center.

GPS Coordinates: 32.1291° N, 104.5539° W

Did You Know?
Carlsbad Cavern is a limestone cave that is actually a fossilized reef that was part of an inland sea that existed about 265 million years ago. Additionally, Indigenous Americans lived within the Guadalupe Mountains and the remains of their cooking rings and pictographs can be found around the park boundaries. The museum within the park has over a million cultural artifacts that are currently being preserved.

This park has two popular historic districts: The Caverns Historic District and the Rattlesnake Springs Historic District.

Journal:

Date(s) Visited:

Weather
conditions:

Who you were with:

Nature observations:

Special memories:

Roswell

Roswell is a city in New Mexico that is situated at the convergence of the Spring, Hondo, and Pecos Rivers. Originally home to the Mescalero Apaches and the hunting grounds of the Comanche tribes, Roswell was officially established by Van Smith in 1870.

Today, Roswell features many art pieces, history, and even the International UFO Museum that is home to The Alien Caffeine Espresso Bar.

Best time to visit:
The best times to visit Roswell are late spring and the fall because the weather will be dry and mild. In the summer, temperatures get hot, and the winters may be cooler.

Pass/Permit/Fees:
There are no fees to enter Roswell, but you may have to pay to visit the museums.

Closest city or town: Roswell, New Mexico

How to get there:
The best ways to get to Roswell are by bus, plane, or car. While flying is the fastest, you'll likely take I-25, I-40, or I-20 West, depending on where you are coming from. For the best directions to Roswell, visitors should input Roswell, New Mexico, into their GPS. You will then get your best route.

GPS Coordinates: 33.3943° N, 104.5230° W

Did You Know?
Roswell is the site of numerous UFO sightings and unexplainable incidents, such as the time a farmer found unidentifiable debris in his sheep pasture that supposedly belonged to the government-based Project Mogul. Roswell is the UFO capital of the world and will be hosting annual UFO festivals starting in 2021.

Journal:

Date(s) Visited:

Weather
conditions:

Who you were with:

Nature observations:

Special memories:

Bisti/De-Na-Zin Badlands

The Bisti/De-Na-Zin Badlands is a wilderness area that features numerous unique, natural structures. Nature has truly shaped the structures of Bisti/De-Na-Zin Badlands in a way that makes visitors think they've entered a completely new world. The rock formations are made of interbedded sandstone, shale, mudstone, coal, and silt and form pinnacles, spires, cap rocks, and other breathtaking and seemingly impossible forms. This wilderness area offers camping, rock climbing, mountain biking, hiking, horseback riding, and beautiful scenery.

Best time to visit:
The park is open year-round, but most visitors come in the late spring and fall to enjoy the best weather.

Pass/Permit/Fees:
There are no fees to enter the park, but permits are required for scenic research and commercial guiding.

Closest city or town: Farmington, NM

How to get there:
To get to the Bisti parking area, visitors should drive on NM-371 around 36 miles south of Farmington or around 45 miles north of Crownpoint and turn east on Road 7297 for two miles. Once you get to the T-intersection, turn left and drive one mile to the parking area.

GPS Coordinates: 36.2921° N, 108.1298° W

Did You Know?
The word "Bisti" means "a large area of shale hills" in the Navajo language, and "De-Na-Zin" comes from the Navajo word for "cranes." This wilderness area has been around for thousands of years and features hundreds of fossils in its sedimentary landforms. While you may find these fossils on your trip, you aren't allowed to remove them.

Journal:

Date(s) Visited:

Weather
conditions:

Who you were with:

Nature observations:

Special memories:

Bandelier National Monument

With a plethora of wildlife and hiking trails for all abilities, the Bandelier National Monument is a great place for all to visit. There are over 70 miles of backpacking trails in the park that go through canyons and mesas.

Best time to visit:
The best time to visit is in the late spring and fall. You'll experience mild weather and minimal storms.

Pass/Permit/Fees:
While some holidays will have free entrance days, Bandelier normally charges $25 per vehicle, $20 per motorcycle, or $15 per individual. A permit is required for overnight stays.

Closest city or town: Los Alamos, NM

How to get there:
Take NM-285 to US-84 in Pojoaque, NM, then go west on NM-502 and west on NM-4 to White Rock. From there, the national monument entrance will be 12 miles and on the south side of the road.

GPS Coordinates: 35.7647° N, 106.3228° W

Did You Know?
Bandelier is home to many animals and a range of ecosystems. Visitors may see mule deer, bighorn sheep, mountain lions, black bears, bobcats, Abert's squirrels, a variety of lizards, rattlesnakes, and numerous year-round and migratory birds. On warm fall days, you may even see a tarantula crossing the path ahead of you. So, make sure to bring your camera.

For over 10,000 years, people—such as the Ancestral Pueblo people—have lived in the Pajarito Plateau and have left their marks on the landscape. Visitors can see the remains of Tyuonyi, Long House, Alcove House, and Talus House in the park.

Journal:

Date(s) Visited:

Weather
conditions:

Who you were with:

Nature observations:

Special memories:

Ruidoso

Ruidoso, New Mexico, is a small mountain town in the Sierra Blanca Mountains. First inhabited by the Mescalero Apache, the area was named Rio Ruidoso by Spanish settlers, which literally translates to "noisy river." The town itself is deeply rooted in Native American culture and offers horseback riding, hiking, camping, and rustic cabins for glamorous camping.

Best time to visit:
There are things to do at all times of the year. Visitors can hike or camp in the summer and ski or take sleigh rides when there is snow. For winter travel, Ruidoso visitor guides recommend 4-wheel drive and chains in case of a winter storm. There generally is rain in the spring and fall, and April and May can get a bit windy.

Pass/Permit/Fees:
There is no fee to enter Ruidoso, but you will need to pay for the attractions.

Closest city or town: Ruidoso, NM

How to get there:
Ruidoso is about 70 miles west of Roswell if you take US Highway 70. If you're coming from the south, the best way to get to Ruidoso is going north on Highway 54 to Tularosa. From the north, visitors should travel south on I-25 until you reach Highway 380. For the most accurate instructions, input Ruidosa, NM, into a GPS.

GPS Coordinates: 33.3673° N, 105.6588° W

Did You Know?
When visiting Ruidoso, you can visit the many cultural and historical attractions, such as the counties where Billy the Kid roamed. Additionally, you can glide down one of the longest ziplines in the world, an 8,900-foot zipline at Ski Apache. There are also numerous casinos and performing arts centers.

Journal:

Date(s) Visited:

Weather conditions:

Who you were with:

Nature observations:

Special memories:

Taos Ski Valley

Taos Ski Valley is a popular ski resort known for Kachina Peak, a mountain that reaches 12,481 feet above sea level. In the winter, you'll find diverse ski trails that range from beginner to intermediate trails. Additionally, you'll find well-groomed trails, glades, moguls, and bowls with some of the lightest powder in all of North America. In the summer, Taos Ski Valley offers hiking, biking, climbing, fishing, and a range of activities.

Best time to visit:
There are both winter and summer activities at Taos Ski Valley, but if you're planning to ski, you'll want to go in the winter months, which are December through March. For summer activities, visit during the spring and fall for the mildest weather.

Pass/Permit/Fees:
Tickets for the ski village cost between $65 and $85 for non-lift tickets and $90 to $128 for peak lift tickets.

Closest city or town: Taos, NM

How to get there:
While there is an airport in Taos Ski Valley, there are also several buses and shuttles. If you're driving, you can get to the Ski Valley by traveling north on US-64 and turning right at the intersection of US-64, NM-522, and NM-150 onto NM-150.

GPS Coordinates: 36.5960° N, 105.4545° W

Did You Know?
In the 1800s, Taos Ski Valley was home to a small copper mining town known as Twining. Nowadays, there are about 34,000 people living in Taos County. Additionally, the Kachina lift goes the highest of any triple chair lift in North America.

Journal:

Date(s) Visited:

Weather
conditions:

Who you were with:

Nature observations:

Special memories:

Wildlife West Nature Park

Wildlife West Nature Park is a 122-acre wildlife refuge near Albuquerque, New Mexico. Because it's a wildlife refuge and rescue, this attraction features over 20 animals that are native to New Mexico. For example, visitors may see cougars, wolves, bears, elk, deer, javelina, fox, raptors, and much more. They do offer overnight excursions, but these are only available by appointment.

Best time to visit:
The park is open from 10 a.m. to 6 p.m. from March 15th through the end of October and has limited hours from November through mid-March. So, the best time to visit is during the spring through fall.

Pass/Permit/Fees:
Admission to the park costs $9 for adults, $7 for seniors, $5 for students, and children under five are free.

Closest city or town: Albuquerque, NM

How to get there:
The best way to get to Wild West Nature Park is to take I-40 to exit 187 (Edgewood) and turn north at the end of the exit. From there, go left at the Conoco station heading west on the North Frontage Road, and keep driving until you see the park entrance on the right. It should be about 20 minutes from Albuquerque.

GPS Coordinates: 35.0696° N, 106.2054° W

Did You Know?
If you're interested, you can rent out the entire park for large events, such as weddings, family reunions, corporate events, and more. When you rent it out, you'll get the entire park to yourself, plus wagon rides, private animal shows, and several activities for young children.

Journal:

Date(s) Visited:

Weather
conditions:

Who you were with:

Nature observations:

Special memories:

Guadalupe Backcountry Scenic Byway

The Guadalupe Backcountry Scenic Byway is a 30-mile road that goes west from the Chihuahuan Desert to the Guadalupe Escarpment. While driving on this scenic byway, visitors will see the vast deserts littered with cactus and dense pines. Not only that, but you may see mule deer, pronghorn antelope, gray fox, scaled quail, mourning dove, songbirds, and other small mammals.

Best time to visit:
The scenic byway is open year-round, so you can drive this gorgeous road any time of year and remain comfortable in your temperature-controlled car. Try driving on the road at sunrise or sunset to get the most spectacular views. Also, always check the weather for storms so that you make the most of your drive.

Pass/Permit/Fees:
There are no fees to use the scenic byway.

Closest city or town: Carlsbad, NM

How to get there:
The Guadalupe Backcountry Scenic Byway is just 12 miles north of Carlsbad, NM, and 23 miles south of Artesia, NM. When you are trying to get to the Byway, look for the signs on US-285 that will direct you there. The entrance is at the intersection of US-285 and State Highway 137 (also known as Queen Highway).

GPS Coordinates: 32.51512778, -104.3798425

Did You Know?
There are many attractions to stop and visit along the drive, such as the Carlsbad Caverns and Lechugilla Cave. There are also many trails to stop at for hiking, backpacking, camping, mountain biking, caving, and more.

Journal:

Date(s) Visited:

Weather conditions:

Who you were with:

Nature observations:

Special memories:

Bisti Badlands

The Bisti Badlands is about 60 square miles of remote landscapes and badlands. Featuring some of the most unique natural structures in the world, visitors can enjoy miles of hiking, exploring wildlife viewing, camping, and exceptional opportunities for photography. Additionally, visitors may have the opportunity to identify fossils and petrified wood.

Best time to visit:
The park is open year-round, but the best time to visit if you want to encounter mild weather is during the late spring and fall.

Pass/Permit/Fees:
There are no fees to enter the park, but permits are required for scenic research and commercial guiding.

Closest city or town: Farmington, NM

How to get there:
To get to the Bisti Badlands, take the gravel Road 7297 off of Highway 371, which is south of Farmington.

GPS Coordinates: 36.2921° N, 108.1298° W

Did You Know?
The "Bisti Beast" is a fossil of an early ancestral relative of the Tyrannosaurus rex. The *Bistahiaversor Sealey* was found by Paul Sealey in 1997, and nearly 60 percent of the skeleton has been preserved. This 30-foot-tall tyrannosaur lived around 74 million years ago and to this day has only ever been found in New Mexico. Many other fossilized dinosaur skeletons have been found in the park, such as the duck-billed Parasaurolophus, Pentaceratops, and a large sauropod known as the Alamosaurus.

Journal:

Date(s) Visited:

Weather conditions:

Who you were with:

Nature observations:

Special memories:

Ojo Caliente Mineral Springs

The healing power of water has been recognized by multiple cultures throughout the world. You can visit this 1,100-acre health resort for a relaxing experience, complete with a full-service spa that offers restorative therapy, massage, mud area, and other body treatments. Additionally, the Artesian Restaurant and Wine Bar feature dishes with Ojo's own herbs, fruits, and vegetables.

Best time to visit:
Ojo Caliente is open year-round, so visitors can visit whenever they are exploring the area. There are also camping and RV parks available that would be best to use in the spring and summer.

Pass/Permit/Fees:
Treatments and amenities cost between $12 and $55, and entrance into the Mineral Springs costs up to $38 per person.

Closest city or town: Santa Fe, NM

How to get there:
If you are coming from the airport or Santa Fe, it's best to take I-25 north to US-285 north. You'll take the bypass road when you approach Santa Fe and follow US-285 until Exit 414. Otherwise, inputting the address into GPS has reportedly worked well.

GPS Coordinates: 36.3043° N, 106.0524° W

Did You Know?
Ojo Caliente Mineral Springs is one of the oldest natural wellness resorts in the United States. It opened its doors in 1868, but its waters have been thought to hold curative powers for thousands of years by Indigenous groups. Moreover, Ojo Caliente is the only hot springs in the world that use four distinct sulfur-free mineral waters.

Journal:

Date(s) Visited:

Weather
conditions:

Who you were with:

Nature observations:

Special memories:

Kasha-Katuwe Tent Rocks National Monument

Kasha-Katuwe Tent Rocks National Monument is an outdoor laboratory that provides opportunities for visitors to learn about how the landscapes were shaped and developed. The two trails at Kasha-Katuwe are for foot traffic only and allow for excellent hiking, birdwatching, and scenic views. There are some unique rock structures and a plethora of interesting plants to identify.

Best time to visit:
The summer months are the most popular time to visit Kasha-Katuwe, but the park is open year-round. In the summer, there may be less parking than during other times of the year.

Pass/Permit/Fees:
There is a $5 fee for private vehicles to enter the park.

Closest city or town: Albuquerque, NM

How to get there:
If you take the GPS directions, you'll go through tribal lands that do not have access to the park. So to get to Kasha-Katuwe, take I-25 and use the exit for Santo/Domingo/Cochiti Lake Reservation Area (Exit 259). From there, follow the signs on NM-22 to get to Cochiti Pueblo and Kasha-Katuwe Tent Rocks National Monument.

GPS Coordinates: 35.6143° N, 106.3583° W

Did You Know?
The rock formation in Kasha-Katuwe was formed by volcanic activity that occurred nearly six to seven million years ago. These eruptions left pumice, ash, and tuff deposits that are over 1,000 feet thick in some places. Further, the volcanic activity left huge rock fragments scattered around the land. In some places, these tent rocks are up to 90 feet tall and are starting to disintegrate because their tents have lost their weather-resistant caprocks.

Journal:

Date(s) Visited:

Weather
conditions:

Who you were with:

Nature observations:

Special memories:

Petroglyph National Monument

Petroglyph National Monument is the site of one of the largest collections of petroglyphs in North America. The symbols and carvings protected by the park are between 400 and 700 years old and were carved by both Indigenous Americans and Spanish settlers. In the park, visitors can go to Boca Negra Canyon, Rinconada Canyon, or Piedras Marcadas Canyon to see these ancient carvings. Additionally, you can hike around the site of cinder cone volcanoes.

Best time to visit:
The fall and spring will have the mildest weather, but the summer temperatures will be between 89 and 99°F.

Pass/Permit/Fees:
There is a $1 parking fee on weekdays and a $2 parking fee on weekends. Otherwise, there are no entrance fees into the park.

Closest city or town: Albuquerque, NM

How to get there:
From I-40, visitors should take Unser Blvd. (Exit 154) and go north 3 miles to Western Trail. After turning west on Western Trail, follow the road until you reach the visitor's center.

From I-25, take Paseo del Norte (Exit 232) and go west towards Coors Road. Continue south on Coors Road to Western Trail. Western Trail will take you to the parking lot and visitor's center.

GPS Coordinates: 35.1368° N, 106.7405° W

Did You Know?
The Volcano Day Use Area is comprised of three separate trails: Volcanoes Trail, JA Volcano, and Albuquerque Overlook; and Vulcan Volcano Loop. Dogs are allowed at the Volcano Day Use Area as long as they are on a leash, and their owners pick up after their waste.

Journal:

Date(s) Visited:

Weather conditions:

Who you were with:

Nature observations:

Special memories:

Continental Divide National Scenic Trail

The Continental Divide National Scenic Trail spans many states across the United States and follows the footsteps of ancient traders who traveled miles to sell their goods. There are 775 miles of completed trail systems in New Mexico that go through Big Hatchet Mountains Wilderness, the Gila Wilderness, the Aldo Leopold Wilderness, El Malpais, the Rio Puerco, the Chama River, and San Pedro Parks before diverging into the Rocky Mountains.

Best time to visit:
The best time to hike the Continental Divide is in the fall (Mid-September/October/November) because these will be the driest months and the safest to hike as there is little likelihood of rain.

Pass/Permit/Fees:
No permits are required for much of the trail, but camping and hiking in state parks, such as the Rockies, require a permit.

Closest city or town: Lordsburg, NM

How to get there:
The most common starting point in New Mexico is the Crazy Cook Monument. Columbus, NM even provides a shuttle service to this starting point, which is the best option for those who are planning to hike the entire trail. To get to the starting point, first get to Lordsburg by I-10. It's 100 miles from there to Crazy Cook, but it's not recommended to drive without a full tank because there are few gas stations.

GPS Coordinates: 31.4970° N, 108.2087° W

Did You Know?
The Continental Divide Trail, also known as the CDT, was first established by Congress in 1978 and spanned 3,100 miles across the United States. The trail goes through several different biospheres, from the cold tundra to the arid desert. There are many attractions and sites to explore along the trail, and you may even encounter mountain lions, bears, and moose in this month-long backpacking experience.

Journal:

Date(s) Visited:

Weather
conditions:

Who you were with:

Nature observations:

Special memories:

Red River Ski and Summer Area

While the Red River Ski and Summer Area is a great ski resort and has snowshoeing and cross-country ski trails in the winter, in the summer, there are many activities to do, such as hiking, backpacking, and horseback riding. When you are on the trails, you will see breathtaking views of the Sangre de Cristo Mountains and the southern part of the Rocky Mountains.

Best time to visit:
Because there are activities to do in both seasons, you can go during the winter months to ski and during the summer for other family-friendly activities.

Pass/Permit/Fees:
Lift tickets cost up to $90 for skiing, and summer activity passes are generally around $25 per person. Otherwise, hiking is free for all.

Closest city or town: Red River, NM

How to get there:
There is no airport in Red River, so visitors will have to get there by car or public transportation. Red River sits on Highway 38, so the best way to get to Red River is to input the directions into GPS and drive through the mountains.

GPS Coordinates: 36.7062° N, 105.4129° W

Did You Know?
Red River was once home to the Ute and Jicarilla Apache tribes. In the 19th century, the Red River was known as River City and was favored by explorers, fur traders, and prospectors. The mountains were heavy with gold, silver, and copper mines, so many people traveled far and wide to settle in the area. The town of River City had its own red-light district, a dozen saloons, a dancing hall, and boarding houses.

In the summer, you can also go ziplining and partake in numerous other family-friendly activities that are offered by the resort.

Journal:

Date(s) Visited:

Weather
conditions:

Who you were with:

Nature observations:

Special memories:

Wheeler Peak

Located in Sangre De Cristo, Wheeler Peak is the highest point and has the highest elevation in New Mexico. The trail that leads to the top of Wheeler Peak is Wheeler Peak Summit Trail #67 in Carson National Forest. The trail begins at 10,200 feet and ends at the summit of Wheeler Peak at 13,161 feet. In the 2.2 miles (after the 4.1 miles traveled on Williams Lake Trailhead) that it takes to get to the top of Wheeler Peak, visitors will experience many mountain switchbacks, and the trail will become narrow at some points. This hike is rated as Intermediate to Expert and may not be suitable for beginner hikers.

Best time to visit:
The best times to visit are the late spring/early summer and fall to avoid the worst of the storms and monsoon season. However, late May through November should be okay to climb, but plan your trip in the morning to avoid afternoon storms.

Pass/Permit/Fees:
No fees are required to use the hiking trail.

Closest city or town: Taos Ski Valley, NM

How to get there:
To find Williams Lake Trailhead, go four miles north on US HWY-64 from Taos to NM HWY-150, then east on HYW-150 to Taos Ski Valley. Go left to Twinning road and follow the signs for Williams Lake Trailhead and Bavarian Lodge and Restaurant. Use the parking lot before Bavarian.

GPS Coordinates: 36.5569° N, 105.4168° W

Did You Know?
Wheeler Peak is named after the US Army Major George M. Wheeler, who did a lot of the surveying of New Mexico in the 1870s. It is not known who made the first complete climb of Wheeler Peak, but it was most likely the Taos Pueblo tribes who have historically inhabited the land.

Journal:

Date(s) Visited:

Weather conditions:

Who you were with:

Nature observations:

Special memories:

Ghost Ranch

From art tours featuring the work of Georgia O'Keeffe to a wellness retreat, to dinosaurs, Ghost Ranch has it all. Not only does Ghost Ranch have an on-site campsite, but it has rustic-style lodging accommodations as well. Visitors can go on guided hikes across the landscape, get a massage in the wellness center, visit the Ruth Hall Museum of Paleontology, or even take a sunset trail ride on horseback.

Best time to visit:
If you visit in the fall, you'll get some of the mildest weather, but many visitors also go during late spring and summer. Because New Mexico stays rather warm year-round, you can go during the winter as well.

Pass/Permit/Fees:
Visitors at Ghost Ranch will pay for each activity as well as their accommodations.

Closest city or town: Abiquiu, NM

How to get there:
Ghost Ranch is 65 miles northwest of Santa Fe if you take US-84. The exit can be found between mile markers 224 and 225. For those who are coming north from Espanola, remain on US-84 until Abiquiu Reservoir, then turn right at the gate about 7-10 minutes after driving past the lake.

GPS Coordinates: 36.3137° N, 106.4820° W

Did You Know?
Many dinosaur fossils have been found in the dinosaur quarry at Ghost Ranch. In fact, archeologists have uncovered some of the world's largest dinosaur fossil collections, and it holds the location of the only complete *Coelophysis,* which happens to be New Mexico's state fossil.

Journal:

Date(s) Visited:

Weather
conditions:

Who you were with:

Nature observations:

Special memories:

Living Desert State Park

Living Desert State Park is meant to resemble the Chihuahuan Desert and features over 40 native animal species in its indoor and outdoor living museum. The self-guided tour is approximately 1.3 miles and takes about an hour and a half to complete. While on the tour, visitors will see hundreds of succulents, sand dunes, and mountainous views. The park has several attractions, such as Birds to Bison, Never Cry Wolf and the Green House.

Best time to visit:
The park is open year-round, but many people visit in late spring through fall for the best weather. However, it can be hot during the summer, and thunderstorms may occur.

Pass/Permit/Fees:
The entrance charge is $5 per vehicle to enter the park.

Closest city or town: Carlsbad, NM

How to get there:
Living Desert Zoo and Gardens State Park can be found on the northwest side of Carlsbad if you take US-285.

GPS Coordinates: 32.4419° N, 104.2781° W

Did You Know?
The Living Desert is modeled after the Chihuahuan Desert, which covers around 250,000 square miles. This desert is unique because about 9,000 years ago, the area was wet and covered in thick forests. When the area started to become drier, some plant species adapted, and others went extinct. This led to the unique plants that are seen in the desert today.

Journal:

Date(s) Visited:

Weather conditions:

Who you were with:

Nature observations:

Special memories:

Blue Hole

Blue Hole, originally known as Blue Lake, is a geographical wonder that was created during a phenomenon known as the Santa Rosa sink. The lake itself is one of seven lakes that are connected via an underground water system. Because it sits in the middle of an arid desert with little water around it, Nomadic tribes, cowboys, and travelers alike visited this oasis. Nowadays, visitors can swim, dive, and jump into Blue Hole on a hot summer's day.

Best time to visit:
The summer is the best time to visit because the water at Blue Hole is cold and will be refreshing in the summer heat.

Pass/Permit/Fees:
The entrance fee is $20 per person.

Closest city or town: Santa Rosa, NM

How to get there:
Blue Hole is located off Route 66 in New Mexico. The easiest way to get to Blue Hole is to take I-40 and get off at Exit 275, then follow the signs to Blue Hole.

GPS Coordinates: 34.9404° N, 104.6732° W

Did You Know?
The visibility through the Blue Hole's water is nearly 100 feet because the water is replaced on its own every six hours. The hole itself is 81 feet deep and has a diameter of 60 feet. Even though the hole becomes a new lake four times a day, the temperature of the water always remains 62°F.

Journal:

Date(s) Visited:

Weather
conditions:

Who you were with:

Nature observations:

Special memories:

Chaco Culture National Historical Park

Chaco Culture National Historical Park features many self-guided tours of cultural and natural sites, including Una Vida, Hungo Pavi, Pueblo Bonito, Chetro Ketl, Pueblo del Arroyo, and Casa Rinconada. The park has many nature trails for hiking, and on the trails, you'll see ancient roads, petroglyphs, stairways, and overlooks of the valley.

Best time to visit:
While the park is open year-round, the best times to visit are the spring and fall because of the moderate temperatures. The summers reach 80 to 90°F, and the winters may have nights that dip below freezing temperatures.

Pass/Permit/Fees:
It costs $25 for a vehicle to enter the park, $20 for a motorcycle, and $15 for an individual.

Closest city or town: Farmington, NM

How to get there:
The park can only be accessed by driving on dirt roads, and some of the roads recommended by GPS may not be safe for some cars. From the north side of New Mexico, turn off US-550 at CR-7900. The south can access the park from HWY-9. For other directional information and road conditions, call ahead.

GPS Coordinates: 36.0530° N, 107.9559° W

Did You Know?
This historical site has massive cultural significance. Chaco Canyon has more than 4,000 prehistoric and historic archaeological sites that showcase more than 10,000 years of human history. Some of these sites preserve early civilization, 16 great houses, prehistoric trade networks, and more.

Journal:

Date(s) Visited:

Weather
conditions:

Who you were with:

Nature observations:

Special memories:

Nambe Falls

Nambe Falls is a series of two waterfalls that are 75 feet and 100 feet tall, respectively. From the short trails, you can see the beautiful waterfalls as well as the Pueblo of Nambe, which manages the trails and surrounding area of Nambe Falls. At the falls, there are opportunities to hike, swim, fish for cutthroat trout and salmon, picnic, and go camping. There are hiking trails below the falls and to an overlook, and all the trails provide beautiful scenery. Visitors have reported that it takes about two to three hours to explore the entire site.

Best time to visit:
The mildest temperatures will be in the spring and fall, but visiting the falls in the summer may be better for water activities.

Pass/Permit/Fees:
It costs $15 for admission into the falls.

Closest city or town: Santa Fe, NM

How to get there:
Nambe Falls is located about 18 miles north of Santa Fe if you take US-84 to State 503 and Nambe Rt. 1. You'll find the entrance to the trail at the ranger's station.

GPS Coordinates: 35.8456° N, 105.9064° W

Did You Know?
Further downstream, you'll find a manmade dam. The United States government began construction on the Nambe Falls Dam in 1974 and completed it in 1976. About 300 miles upstream of Nambe Falls, the dam is a 150-foot-tall concrete structure that provides water for Pojoaque Valley Irrigation District and the pueblos of San Ildefonso, Nambe, and Pojoaque.

Journal:

Date(s) Visited:

Weather conditions:

Who you were with:

Nature observations:

Special memories:

Catwalk Trail Falls

Catwalk Trail Falls is a trail that goes along an 1890's mining waterway and traverses through many historical sites. Part of the Gila National Forest, the entrance to the Catwalk Trail is also called Catwalk National Recreation #207 Trail. The trail goes for about 1.5 miles and features hidden pools and gorgeous waterfalls, and leads to the more rigorous trails of the Gila Wilderness.

Best time to visit:
The most popular time to visit is during the summer, but the mildest weather will be in the spring and fall. Before you go, however, check with the Forest Service for weather and trail conditions to make sure it's safe.

The trail is typically open from dawn to dusk, but it can also be a heavily used trail during popular hiking times.

Pass/Permit/Fees:
There is a $3 parking fee to hike the Catwalk Trail.

Closest city or town: Glenwood, NM

How to get there:
To get to the Catwalk Trail, drive five miles away from Glenwood to Catwalk Road. The area is at the very end of Highway 174.

GPS Coordinates: 33.372555° N 108.841735° W

Did You Know?
The Catwalk was originally named for the plank-board walkway that was on top of the steel pipe that once brought water down to an ore processing plant. Even though nearly all the pipe is now gone, most of the modern hiking trail follows the same route. So while you're hiking, keep an eye out for the remains of the old pipe.

Journal:

Date(s) Visited:

Weather conditions:

Who you were with:

Nature observations:

Special memories:

Sitting Bull Falls

Sitting Bull Falls is a series of waterfalls, streams, and pools located in Lincoln National Forest. Once the water leaves the falls, it disappears between the gravel, cracks, and rocks and reappears further downstream or becomes part of the Pecos Valley underground water reserve. This 150-foot-tall waterfall is a rare find in an arid desert, and the recreation area offers cool pools, pavilions, picnic areas, charcoal grills, and many outdoor activities such as hiking, biking, and horseback riding. There is a paved trail that leads to the falls as well as 16 miles worth of canyon trails for all outdoor activities.

Best time to visit:
The busiest season for Sitting Bull Falls is the summer, but the mildest weather is in the spring and fall.

Pass/Permit/Fees:
The fee to enter Sitting Bull Falls Recreation Area is $5 per vehicle per day.

Closest city or town: Carlsbad, NM

How to get there:
The best way to get to Sitting Bull Falls is to go north from Carlsbad and turn west onto NM-137. After 20 miles on NM-137, turn right on CR-149. At the end of the road will be the recreation area.

GPS Coordinates: 32.2432° N, 104.6963° W

Did You Know?
While no one knows exactly how Sitting Bull Falls got its name, it has been suspected that the falls were named after a well-known Sioux medicine man. However, the Apache tribes named the area *gostahanagunti*, which translates to "hidden gulf" in English.

Journal:

Date(s) Visited:

Weather
conditions:

Who you were with:

Nature observations:

Special memories:

Folsom Falls

Folsom Falls is one of three small waterfalls that are part of the Dry Cimarron River. They are currently located on private land, and visitors are warned not to trespass. For years, the area was open to the public and is now managed and leased by New Mexico Fish and Wildlife. But, if you take the Dry Cimarron Scenic Byway, you'll eventually come across Folsom Falls. There is a small area for parking off the side of the road, and you'll have to get through the gates to get to the falls. From the gate, they are only a couple of hundred yards away.

Best time to visit:
Available to be viewed year-round, the best time to visit would be during New Mexico's hot summer.

Pass/Permit/Fees:
There are no fees to get to the falls, but the falls are currently on private land owned by New Mexico Fish and Wildlife.

Closest city or town: Folsom, NM

How to get there:
To get to Folsom Falls, travel northeast of Folsom, New Mexico, on Highway 456. From there, you'll go four miles to reach the falls.

GPS Coordinates: 36.8728° N, 103.8808° W

Did You Know?
Folsom Falls is a favorite fishing spot and scenic picnicking area. While the waterfalls themselves are not huge, they still offer the beautiful sound of rushing water. However, it's not recommended to swim at Folsom Falls because the current can get too strong.

Journal:

Date(s) Visited:

Weather conditions:

Who you were with:

Nature observations:

Special memories:

Soda Dam

The Soda Dam is a 7,000-year-old natural bridge that is made from calcium carbonate. This odd geographic structure is actually a hot springs deposit, and before State Route 4 was built, it was getting bigger every year. Unfortunately, the road destroyed part of the dam and re-routed its natural water flow, so the dam is slowly disintegrating. However, that does not stop visitors from far and wide from visiting this 300-foot-long natural dam that is also over 50 feet tall.

Best time to visit:
You can visit the Soda Dam any time as it's open year-round. However, the best driving conditions are in the late spring through fall.

Pass/Permit/Fees:
There are currently no fees to visit the geological structure.

Closest city or town: Jemez Springs, NM

How to get there:
Getting to the Soda Dam is simple and can easily be accessed from State Highway 4. The site is a few miles north of Jemez Springs. However, be careful when parking along the shoulder of the road.

GPS Coordinates: 35.7920° N, 106.6866° W

Did You Know?
The substance that makes up the Soda Dam, calcium carbonate, is the same substance that is found in eggshells, snail shells, and pearls. It's a very common mineral and is naturally found in limestone, calcite, and aragonite. In fact, it makes up 4% of the Earth's crust. Additionally, calcium carbonate can be used as chalk for writing purposes, as a dietary supplement, and as an antacid to relieve stomach pain. All in all, it's quite a versatile substance.

Journal:

Date(s) Visited:

Weather conditions:

Who you were with:

Nature observations:

Special memories:

White Rock Overlook Park Waterfall

White Rock Overlook Park is one of the parks located near White Rock and Los Alamos. The waterfall on the White Rock trail is part of a 7.8-mile trail system. It's a small 7-foot dual waterfall that seemingly pops out of nowhere when you are on the trail. To get to the waterfalls, you will take the Red Dot or Blue Dot Trail and go through White Rock Canyon along the Rio Grande River. You will also see petroglyphs, springs, and an abundance of wildlife.

Best time to visit:
The spring or fall will have the mildest weather, but you can hike the trail in the summer. The summer will get hot, however, so bring plenty of water as there is not much shade on the trail.

Pass/Permit/Fees:
There are no fees to park or hike the trailheads.

Closest city or town: White Rock, NM

How to get there:
The Red Dot and Blue Dot Trails are both on State Road 4. To get to the Blue Dot Trailhead, turn on Rover Blvd.; to get to the Red Dot Trailhead, continue farther down State Road 4 and turn left on Sherwood.

GPS Coordinates: 35.48143 ° N, 106.11722° W

Did You Know?
The trail is called the Red Dot (or Blue Dot) Trail because there are spray-painted dots that line the trail. These red dots make sure hikers do not get lost along their way because the trail can be hard to follow at times. So if you are traveling to White Rock Overlook or the waterfalls, follow the red or blue dots.

Journal:

Date(s) Visited:

Weather
conditions:

Who you were with:

Nature observations:

Special memories:

Bar Canyon-Soledad Canyon Waterfall

For gorgeous views of the Organ Mountains and Mesilla Valley, hike the three-mile loop of the Bar Canyon Trail. Depending on how much rainfall there has been, the waterfall you will pass on the trail can range from a slight trickle to a massive stream that runs into a small pond. To get to the waterfall, you will have to deviate from the main trail, but it is not a far walk. Not only can you hike, bike, or travel the trail by horseback, but the Soledad Canyon Lookout is known for its wildlife viewing.

Best time to visit:
While the park is open year-round, the best times to visit are during the spring and fall because these times will likely have the driest and mildest temperatures. However, the summer is also a popular time to hike to see the waterfall.

Pass/Permit/Fees:
There are no fees to hike the trails.

Closest city or town: Las Cruces, NM

How to get there:
The Bar Canyon Trails are on the west side of the Organ Mountains and are 10 miles east of Las Cruces, NM. The best way to get to the trails is to take Exit 1 on I-25 and take University Avenue/Dripping Springs Road east for 4.5 miles. Then, turn south on Soledad Canyon Road and follow the road until the end to find the trailhead.

GPS Coordinates: 32.306 ° N, 106.589 ° W

Did You Know?
If you take a slight detour off the trail, you will find the remains of a 20th-century homestead. The ruins have been abandoned for nearly 100 years, but the foundation stands to mark its location. Even though the structure is manmade, the Earth has begun to reclaim its resources because much of it is deteriorating.

Journal:

Date(s) Visited:

Weather conditions:

Who you were with:

Nature observations:

Special memories:

Jemez Falls

Located in the Santa Fe National Forest, Jemez Falls is 70 feet high and generally has a healthy flow of water. Jemez Falls are the highest falls in the Jemez Mountains and are an easy quarter-mile hike from the paved parking lot. The trail ends with an overlook of the falls, and visitors should expect to spend about 45 minutes completing the loop. While you can easily get to the overlook from the parking lot, some visitors opt to use the East Fork Trail (four miles round trip) for a more rigorous hike.

Best time to visit:
The best time to visit Jemez Falls is during the summer, but this is also when the trail is the most trafficked.

Pass/Permit/Fees:
There are no fees required to use the trails.

Closest city or town: La Cueva, NM and Jemez Springs, NM

How to get there:
To get to the falls, you will need to take State Road 4 until Forest Rd. 134. Once you turn onto Forest Rd. 134, you will turn onto Forest Rd. 135 for about a mile before turning back on to Forest Rd. 134. The parking lot for Jemez Falls is about a quarter-mile after you make that final turn.

GPS Coordinates: 35.8125° N, 106.6069° W

Did You Know?
Evidence of human life in the Jemez Valley dates back as far as 2500 BC. Archeological findings have been found in the Jemez Canyon and Soda Dam, which indicates that humans have been migrating through the area for thousands of years. Eventually, pueblos were formed, and as many as 30,000 people called the valley home.

Journal:

Date(s) Visited:

Weather conditions:

Who you were with:

Nature observations:

Special memories:

El Salto Falls

El Salto Falls on the El Salto del Agua Cañoncito Trail is just over five miles. The trail is an out and back and is generally lightly trafficked. However, the trail is rated as difficult because there is a 1,040-foot gain in elevation. In fact, it's so difficult that hikers must call the warden (505-398-0090) before coming to the trail. The falls are 200 feet tall and are at nearly 9,000 feet in elevation. El Salto Falls is composed of five separate drops that make for a beautiful and elaborate waterfall.

Best time to visit:
The fall and spring are the best times to visit the falls because the stream that makes up the falls is light and may dry up in the summer.

Pass/Permit/Fees:
There is a $5 fee per person to hike this trail because it is on private land.

Closest city or town: Arroyo Seco, NM

How to get there:
The trail entrance is just two miles from Arroyo Seco, NM. The easiest way to get there is to go southeast on NM-150 towards El Salto Rd. and take a left. Then, turn left on Paw-A-Suki Rd. and you'll arrive at the entrance.

GPS Coordinates: 36.5326° N, 105.5378° W

Did You Know?
The El Salto waterfall is located on private land that is on about 2,000 acres of wilderness and was given to Antonio Martinez in 1716 or 1717. Today, the land is owned by the descendants of the Martinez family, who also manage the land. All the fees that are paid to use the trail go towards maintaining the land.

Journal:

Date(s) Visited:

Weather conditions:

Who you were with:

Nature observations:

Special memories:

Resumidero Falls

Resumidero Falls is comprised of three drops, with the three drops being 30, 15, and 20 feet, respectively. In total, Resumidero Falls is about 70 feet tall. One of the falls is truly unique in that it falls through a hole that has been naturally made in solid granite rock. These falls are an absolute hidden treasure, and some visitors have reported seeing wild horses near the falls.

Best time to visit:
The best times to visit the area are in the summer and fall because the water from the falls is cold. The summers can get hot, so bring water.

Pass/Permit/Fees:
No fees or reservations are required to visit the falls or the camping areas.

Closest city or town: Coyote, NM

How to get there:
To get to the Resumidero camping area and entrance to the San Pedro Parks Wilderness, take SH-96 to FR-103 for about nine miles. Then, turn onto FR-93 and travel for two miles to the camping area.

GPS Coordinates: 36.114451° N, 106.746919° W

Did You Know?
This is not an easy waterfall to get to, but Resumidero Falls is worth the trek. There is no distinct hiking path to the falls, but some have said they had success traveling from Vivian Falls, which is less than half a mile from Resumidero Falls. However, most people reach the falls by hiking south on the Rio Puerco from the Rio Puerco campsite. If you do not start at the campsite, you can access the river from Forest Road 93.

Journal:

Date(s) Visited:

Weather conditions:

Who you were with:

Nature observations:

Special memories:

Williams Falls

The trail leading to Williams Falls offers opportunities to hike, snowshoe, cross country ski, or travel by horseback. Williams Falls is located near Williams Lake and Wheeler Peak, so you will have amazing views as you hike along the trail to this 35-foot-tall waterfall. To access the waterfall, you simply hike down Williams Lake Trail in Carson National Forest. You'll see amazing views of the mountains, towering trees, and an abundance of wildlife.

Best time to visit:
This trail system can be accessed at all times of the year. For hiking or horseback riding, use the trail system during the summer; for cross country skiing and snowshoeing, visit the trail during the winter months.

Pass/Permit/Fees:
There are no fees to hike the trails in Carson National Forest.

Closest city or town: Taos, NM

How to get there:
From Taos, NM, travel four miles north to the intersection of NM-150 and go east to Taos Ski Valley. Then, continue through the ski parking lot and head to the Twining Campground. After turning right onto Twining Road, you'll switch back twice onto Kachina Road. The parking lot is about three miles down that road past the Bavarian Lodge and the Kachina chairlift.

GPS Coordinates: 43.4880° N, 96.7692° W

Did You Know?
Williams Lake is a natural lake, but it does not have any fish in its waters because it completely freezes in the winter. Additionally, the lake is at an elevation of over 11,000 feet, which makes it quite a unique sight for anyone hiking through the mountains.

Journal:

Date(s) Visited:

Weather
conditions:

Who you were with:

Nature observations:

Special memories:

Three Rivers Waterslides

Contrary to its name, Three Rivers Waterslides is actually a small waterfall that flows over smooth rocks. These smooth, clean rocks make this waterfall a natural waterslide. If you do choose to slide, however, know that it will not be the same as a manmade waterslide, and your backside may hurt afterward. The waterslides are at about 7,900 feet of elevation and can be found in the Lincoln National Forest.

Best time to visit:
The best time to visit Three Rivers Waterslides is from May to October because these will be the warmest months. You can hike in the area in the winter, but you would likely need snowshoes, and you wouldn't be able to slide down the rock. The trail is difficult, so bring enough water.

Pass/Permit/Fees:
There are no fees required to hike the trails in Lincoln National Forest.

Closest city or town: Ruidoso, NM

How to get there:
Take US-54 north from Tularosa until Forest Road 579 (16 miles). Then, go 14 miles to Three Rivers Campground. The trailhead is located at the campground and has free parking.

GPS Coordinates: 33.40313 ° N, 105.8548 ° W

Did You Know?
The Three Rivers Waterslides waterfall is part of the 11 miles of trail known as the Three Rivers Trail. Once you have been on the trail for about three miles, you will see the waterfalls on the right side. The trail is rated as difficult because of the length and the total 3,444 feet of elevation that you will traverse. This trail features campsites, creeks, caves, and more. While you are on the trail, you should keep your eyes out for wildlife because many visitors have reported seeing skunks, deer, mountain lions, and more while hiking. This is also a great trail for backpacking because there are many primitive campsites along the trail.

Journal:

Date(s) Visited:

Weather conditions:

Who you were with:

Nature observations:

Special memories:

North Fork Casa Falls

North Fork Casa Falls is a 50-foot-tall waterfall that is part of a series of waterfalls that are about 1,500 feet of cascading waterfalls. Found in the Pecos Wilderness of the Carson National Forest, Casa Falls is the most popular of the falls in this area. There are other falls in the area that you can visit if you are feeling adventurous. You can hike to the falls fairly easily and see an abundance of wildlife along the way. Additionally, there won't be many people on the trails, so you can enjoy nature uninterrupted.

Best time to visit:
May through October are the best times to visit the falls to get the best weather and observe the best water flow.

Pass/Permit/Fees:
There are no fees required to visit the falls.

Closest city or town: Mora, NM

How to get there:
There are very few road signs directing you to the falls. The best way to get to the falls is to go four miles north on NM HWY-518 from Mora and turn west on road B-028 for five miles. You'll find Forest Road #113, which will lead to Walker Flats, which is one mile west of the falls.

GPS Coordinates: 36°00.812° N, 105°28.903° W

Did You Know?
If you are traveling to the falls and happen to get lost on your way, call the Taos Search and Rescue squad. In 2018, an older couple got lost while they were trying to find the falls. The trail to the falls can be tricky to find at some spots, so make sure you bring extra food and water just in case you find yourself off the trail. Luckily, the 60-year-old couple had packed more than enough food, water, and emergency blankets to get them through the night. They were found unharmed by the rescue team and walked back to their car safely.

Journal:

Date(s) Visited:

Weather
conditions:

Who you were with:

Nature observations:

Special memories:

Upper Frijoles Falls

Near the Bandelier National Monument, visitors can take an easy hike along the Frijoles Creek to get to the Upper Frijoles Falls. These falls are 90 feet tall and are just 1.4 miles from the trailhead. While you are hiking the Falls Trail, you'll come across the Tent Rocks that are found around volcanic vents, bushes and agaves, and deep canyons. If you continue your hike, you may also encounter deer, snakes, and many colorful birds.

Best time to visit:
The trails are open all year, but the spring and summer are the most trafficked times due to the warm weather.

Pass/Permit/Fees:
There is a $25 vehicle fee to access Bandelier National Monument.

Closest city or town: Los Alamos, NM

How to get there:
Take NM-285 to US-84 in Pojoaque, NM. From there, go west on NM-4 towards White Rock. The entrance to Bandelier National Monument will be 12 miles down that road.

GPS Coordinates: 35.7634° N, 106.2597° W

Did You Know?
If you continue your hike past the falls, you'll come across ancient Anasazi dwellings that were carved into the landscape. You can also take a path that follows the Rio Grande through White Rock Canyon. If you are feeling particularly adventurous, you can hike to Cochiti Lake, which is about 14 miles from the falls. Along with Cochiti Lake, you'll be near the Cochiti pueblo.

Journal:

Date(s) Visited:

Weather conditions:

Who you were with:

Nature observations:

Special memories:

Fillmore Waterfall New Mexico

The Fillmore Waterfall is 40 feet tall and is found at an elevation of 6,240 feet above sea level. During the winter and early spring, the waterfall flows heavily. But, during the summer, you may get to see the remnants of the slow trickle and pool that is left over from the snowmelt. The waterfall is found in the spectacular Organ Mountains. While on the Fillmore Canyon Trail, you'll see old mining shafts, gorgeous views of the canyon, creeks, and plenty of flora and fauna.

Best time to visit:
The trails are open year-round, but if you want to see heavy water flow and a frothy waterfall, it's best to go in early spring or during the winter. Keep in mind that the trails are only open from 8:00 a.m. until 5:00 p.m.

Pass/Permit/Fees:
There is a $3 fee for a single-day pass for one vehicle.

Closest city or town: Las Cruces, NM

How to get there:
To get to the Fillmore Canyon Trail, you'll want to first drive to the visitor's center. The Dripping Spring Visitor Center is 10 miles east of I-25. Once you take Exit 1, you'll be on the western edge of the Organ Mountains.

GPS Coordinates: 32°20.360'N, 106°34.620'W

Did You Know?
There were many silver and lead mining camps located in the Organ Mountains from 1849 to 1898. In 1898, the Modoc Mining Company invested nearly one million dollars to create a three-story mill that had many shafts, hoists, and tramways. Unfortunately, the mine went bankrupt in 1903 due to a lack of water and other issues. The shafts of this mine can still be found on the Fillmore Canyon Trail, but they have been fenced off so that hikers don't accidentally fall into them.

Journal:

Date(s) Visited:

Weather conditions:

Who you were with:

Nature observations:

Special memories:

Holden Prong Cascades

The Holden Prong Cascades are unique gems when it comes to New Mexico's waterfalls. Situated in the Gila National Forest, the Holden Prong Cascades are a series of waterfalls that are found along the 11-mile Holden Prong Trail No. 114. This trail features a mixture of aspen and mixed conifer forests as well as many small pools and falls. Rated as an intermediate-level trail, you'll experience a 2,460-foot change in elevation and end at 8,700 feet above sea level. Visitors can hike, camp, horseback ride, and backpack along the trail to see its gorgeous views and beautiful landscape.

Best time to visit:
Visitors should plan to hike the cascades during the spring through fall. Winter can have snow which makes the trails difficult to travel.

Pass/Permit/Fees:
No fees are required.

Closest city or town: Kingston, NM

How to get there:
Trail No. 114 does not have a trailhead, so you'll have to follow Trail 129 to Trail 128 (about 4.8 miles). You will follow Trail 128 until trails 128, 79, and 114 intersect. To get to trail No. 129, follow NM-152 for 22.3 miles west of Hillsboro, NM. Look for the trailhead for No. 129 on the right side. From Silver City, go east on NM-152 for 34 miles.

GPS Coordinates: 33.01236° N, 107.74400° W

Did You Know?
There are numerous loops within Holden Prong that are up to 30 miles each. So, there are many opportunities for backpacking and camping. The best camping in Holden Prong is a two-mile area above the confluence of Water Canyon. If you try to camp in the upper section of Holden Prong, you'll run into forests that are too dense to camp in.

Journal:

Date(s) Visited:

Weather conditions:

Who you were with:

Nature observations:

Special memories:

Heron Lake; Rio Arriba County

For some of New Mexico's best fishing, camping, boating, hiking, bird watching, and water activities, you simply must visit Heron Lake State Park in Rio Arriba County. Heron Lake is perfect for kayaking, paddle boarding, and fishing because boats are not allowed to create a wake. Additionally, there are many hiking and cross-country skiing trails around the lake. Heron Lake sits among tall New Mexico pine trees and offers views of the mountainous landscape. There is even a 5.5-mile trail that crosses a large suspension bridge and leads to the nearby lake, El Vado Lake.

Best time to visit:
For water activities, the best time to visit is during the summer. However, you can trek the trails year-round.

Pass/Permit/Fees:
There is a $5 entrance fee per vehicle. Camping and other activities may require additional fees.

Closest city or town: Los Ojos, NM

How to get there:
From Santa Fe, go north on US-84/285 for 22 miles to Espanola, NM. Cross the Rio Grande and continue north towards Abiquiu, Tierra Amarilla, and Chama. You'll continue on US-84 for about 70 miles and turn onto State Road 95. You'll find the entrance to Heron Park on this road in a few miles.

GPS Coordinates: 36.6887° N, 106.6940° W

Did You Know?
Visitors have reported some amazing wildlife around the area, such as mountain lions, black bears, elk, deer, marmots, bald eagles, osprey, and more. Regardless of if you stay for a day or the entire week, you're bound to see some elusive animals and breathtaking views.

Journal:

Date(s) Visited:

Weather
conditions:

Who you were with:

Nature observations:

Special memories:

Turquoise Trail

The Turquoise Trail National Scenic Byway is a 15,000-square-mile historic and scenic area that connects Albuquerque and Santa Fe. As you drive the 50 miles of Highway 14, you'll travel through old mining towns, miles of gorgeous landscape, and many opportunities to get out of the car and explore the trails. Don't forget to bring your camera because you'll have the chance to capture some of New Mexico's most famous scenic views, such as Tijeras, Cedar Crest, Sandia Park, and Cibola National Forest.

Best time to visit:
You can drive along the road year-round but watch for severe weather because you won't want to get caught in a storm. Also, try driving along the road at sunrise or sunset for the most breathtaking views.

Pass/Permit/Fees:
There are no fees required to drive along the scenic byway. Other activities may require additional fees.

Closest city or town: Madrid, NM

How to get there:
If you start in Albuquerque, take I-40 east to the Tijeras exit (175). You'll see the National Scenic Byway sign. From Santa Fe, take NM HWY 14 south and go under I-25.

GPS Coordinates: 35° 24' 21.00" N, 106° 09' 16.19" W

Did You Know?
There are many places to stop and camp along the scenic byway, as well as numerous old mining towns that boast local art, crafts, theater, music, museums, and restaurants. Further, check out the local events of the towns of Golden, Madrid, and Cerrillos because they host many parades and festivals throughout the year.

Journal:

Date(s) Visited:

Weather
conditions:

Who you were with:

Nature observations:

Special memories:

Camel Rock

To see one of New Mexico's most unique rock structures, head to Camel Rock. Camel Rock is exactly what it sounds like: a rock that resembles the shape of a camel. You can easily see this sitting camel from US HWY-285. If you take the exit, you will find a parking area and walking path to the 40-foot-tall and 100-foot-long rock structure. The sandstone that the camel is made of is a light pink and tan color, which adds to its camel-like appearance.

Best time to visit:
You can visit Camel Rock year-round. However, the spring and summer will likely have more visitors.

Pass/Permit/Fees:
No fees are required to visit Camel Rock.

Closest city or town: Pojoque, NM

How to get there:
Go north on US-84/285 out of Santa Fe and drive along the foothills of the Sangre de Cristo Mountains. Camel Rock is near Exit 175, near the Tesuque Pueblo, and across from Camel Rock Casino.

GPS Coordinates: 35.7695° N, 105.9472° W

Did You Know?
In late January or early February of 2017, the Camel's nose came loose and fell off the rock structure. However, the difference is so minute that most visitors wouldn't be able to notice that the camel looks any different. In fact, the structure doesn't look much different and still resembles the shape of a sitting camel.

Journal:

Date(s) Visited:

Weather
conditions:

Who you were with:

Nature observations:

Special memories:

Bosque del Apache National Wildlife Refuge

Established in 1939, the Bosque del Apache National Wildlife Refuge features numerous trails, guided tours, fishing, and more within the 57,331 acres of park. You can choose to hike on the Desert Arboretum, Observation Blind Trail, Boardwalk Trail, Sparrow Loop, John P. Taylor Jr. Memorial Trail, Bajada Loop, Marsh Overlook Trail, and more to see unique wildlife and gorgeous scenery. You'll see reptiles, birds, mammals, and more while exploring these trails. Plus, the wildlife that frequents the park is often seasonal, so you'll see different animals depending on when you visit.

Best time to visit:
The park is open year-round, and visitors can enter between sunrise and sunset.

Pass/Permit/Fees:
There is a $5 entrance fee per vehicle to enter the refuge.

Closest city or town: San Antonio, NM

How to get there:
To get to the visitor's center from the north, drive south on I-25 to Exit 139. Then, go east for 0.25 miles on US-380 and turn right on HWY-1. From the south, drive north on I-25 to Exit 115 and drive west on US-380. Turn north on HWY-1.

GPS Coordinates: 33.8045° N, 106.8911° W

Did You Know?
The Sandhill Crane (*Grus Canadensis*) is a frequent resident of the wildlife refuge. This crane is spotted in the park from late October to about mid-February. They have about ten different calls and do quite elaborate dances for courtship. If you are interested in bird watching, consider visiting the park during the season that these cranes are park residents.

Journal:

Date(s) Visited:

Weather
conditions:

Who you were with:

Nature observations:

Special memories:

Brazos Cliffs

The Brazos Cliffs reach roughly 3,000 feet into the sky at their highest point. While you can no longer climb the Brazos Cliffs because they are currently on private property, you can hike around the area and view its scenic beauty. The best way to hike and view the cliffs is to get on the Tony Marques Trail (#41) in the Carson National Forest. On this trail, you will experience stunning views of the cliffs as well as the Colorado border, Brazos Ridge Mountain Range, Sangre de Cristo Mountains, and more.

Best time to visit:
Spring through fall offers the best weather for hiking.

Pass/Permit/Fees:
The trails are free to hike.

Closest city or town: Los Ojos, NM

How to get there:
The cliffs can be seen if you drive nine miles on US HWY-84 from Chama. The Brazos Cliffs are one mile north of the Brazos River crossing if you go east on NM-512.

GPS Coordinates: 36.7493° N, 106.3936° W

Did You Know?
The rock that makes up the Brazos Cliffs is some of the oldest rock found in the state of New Mexico. The Precambrian quartzite and plutonic rock date back 1.8 billion years. Brazos Cliffs are made from weather-resistant material that has survived the test of time. Additionally, the peak of the Brazos Cliffs is rounded, which also signifies its old age.

The first rock climber to climb the Brazos Cliffs was George Bell in 1952, and he was one of the Los Alamos Mountaineers who helped discover the 45 routes on the cliffs.

Journal:

Date(s) Visited:

Weather conditions:

Who you were with:

Nature observations:

Special memories:

Capulin Volcano National Monument

If you have ever wanted to explore an extinct volcano, here is your chance. Capulin Volcano National Monument is part of an 8,000 square mile volcanic field known as Raton-Clayton. Visitors can hike on the paved Crater Rim Trail or go on the more strenuous trails that wrap around the base of Capulin. Additionally, you can go during Saturday nights in the summer to the Dark Sky stargazing events.

Best time to visit:
The park is open year-round, but the summertime will likely be the busiest. You can also go to the overflow parking lot to view the night sky.

Pass/Permit/Fees:
The park charges a $20 entrance fee per vehicle.

Closest city or town: Capulin, NM

How to get there:
The park is located 33 miles east of Raton, NM, and 57 miles west of Clayton, NM, if you take NM-325 north of US-64.

GPS Coordinates: 36.7811° N, 103.9695° W

Did You Know?
The Capulin Volcano has intrigued nearly every person who has ever come near it. In fact, people far and wide would come to explore the interesting crater and would travel by horse, wagon, car, or foot just to see it for themselves. People have historical connections to Capulin, such as Ernest Thompson Seton, the founder of the Boy Scouts of America, and Jessie Foote Jack, the first female custodian in the National Park Service.

Journal:

Date(s) Visited:

Weather
conditions:

Who you were with:

Nature observations:

Special memories:

Chaco Canyon

Chaco Canyon is the site of numerous historical ruins. In fact, there are ten major sites that visitors can learn about and explore. To see the ruins, visitors can take an eight-mile loop trail that goes right next to these ancient villages. Additionally, the park features four separate trails that explore the entire area. These trails include the Wijiji Trail, South Mesa Trail, Pueblo Alto Trail, and Peñasco Blanco Trail. While the Peñasco Blanco Trail is the one that will take you to the ancient ruins, all the trails feature the gorgeous mesa landscape and Chacoan roads.

Best time to visit:
You can visit the park year-round, but it will be the most trafficked in the summer months.

Pass/Permit/Fees:
The park charges $25 for a vehicle to enter (it lasts up to seven days).

Closest city or town: Bloomfield, NM

How to get there:
There are distinct directions to follow depending on where you are coming from, so make sure to contact the visitor's center for exact directions and road conditions. Simply following a GPS is not advised because the local roads can become unsafe at times.

GPS Coordinates: 36.0530° N, 107.9559° W

Did You Know?
The ruins of Chaco are some of the best-preserved sites of ancient architecture. The ruins were built along the wall of a canyon in the high desert. These ruins feature some very advanced architecture and technology because some are up to five stories high and have hundreds of rooms that people once inhabited.

Journal:

Date(s) Visited:

Weather conditions:

Who you were with:

Nature observations:

Special memories:

Valles Caldera National Preserve

The Valles Caldera is a 13-mile-wide depression in the Earth that was caused by a massive volcanic eruption. This volcano erupted nearly 1.25 million years ago, and since then, the area has become a beautiful area full of mountain meadows, trickling springs, and an abundance of wildlife. The 88,900-acre preserve offers several outdoor activities, such as fishing, hiking, horseback riding, mountain biking, and astronomy. Or, you could look for the preserve's 51 mammal species, 117 bird species, and different types of reptiles, amphibians, and fish species.

Best time to visit:
The park is open year-round, but the summer is the most popular time to visit to preserve.

Pass/Permit/Fees:
Seven-day passes are $25 per vehicle.

Closest city or town: Jemez Springs, NM

How to get there:
From Jemez Springs, take NM-4 north for 22 miles. You will see the main gate around mile marker 39.2. If you are coming from Los Alamos, take Trinity Drive to Diamond. After you take a left on Diamond, take a right on West Jemez Road towards NM-4. Take a right towards the Jemez Mountains and look for the preserve in 18 miles.

GPS Coordinates: 35.8321° N, 106.4870° W

Did You Know?
Native Americans traversed the lands of Valles Caldera National Preserve for thousands of years. Not only did they hunt, fish, and gather food on the land, but the area was known for its obsidian, a substance used to craft many ancient tools.

Journal:

Date(s) Visited:

Weather
conditions:

Who you were with:

Nature observations:

Special memories:

El Morro National Monument

Even though El Morro National Monument is one of New Mexico's smaller national parks, it holds several wonders, beautiful landscapes, and major historical context. You can visit Inscription Rock, the site of over 2,000 drawings that have been inscribed in the sandstone, or you could visit the pool that makes this area so unique. There are two major trails in the park: the Inscription Trail and the Headland Trail. The Inscription Trail heads towards Inscription Rock and the pool, and the Headland Trail explores the volcanic craters of the El Malpais area, El Morro Valley, and the ancient ruins of Astinna.

Best time to visit:
The park is open year-round, but the summer is the most popular time to visit.

Pass/Permit/Fees:
There is no fee to enter the park.

Closest city or town: Grants, NM

How to get there:
From Albuquerque (or from the east), take I-40 west towards Grants. Once you get to Exit 81, go south on HWY-53 for 42 miles. From the west, take I-40 east toward Gallup. Once you come to Exit 20, head south on HWY-602 for 31 miles. Then, turn east on HWY-53, and you will get to El Morro in 25 miles.

GPS Coordinates: 35.0396° N, 108.3451° W

Did You Know?
El Morro is full of sandstone cliffs that hide a deep pool of water. This oasis has been a focal point of weary travels for thousands of years because the pool holds water year-round. Many of these travelers have left their mark on the area via inscriptions in the colorful stone.

Journal:

Date(s) Visited:

Weather conditions:

Who you were with:

Nature observations:

Special memories:

Ah-Shi-Sle-Pah Wilderness

The Ah-Shi-Sle-Pah Wilderness is situated in the northeastern part of New Mexico and is a badlands area full of clay hills. Because of its water-carved hills, the Ah-Shi-Sle-Pah Wilderness does not have much vegetation. Full of spectacular geological structures and formations, this area is also home to many fossils. Even though there are no established trails in the Ah-Shi-Sle-Pah Wilderness, you can still pull your car over on the side of the road and experience the rolling hills, Great Basin scrubland, and grasslands for yourself.

Best time to visit:
You can visit the wilderness area year-round, but the summer will have the warmest temperatures.

Pass/Permit/Fees:
There are no fees required to hike in the wilderness area.

Closest city or town: Farmington, NM

How to get there:
From US HWY-550, go 7.5 miles northwest of Nageezi, NM, and turn left onto NM-57. Head south for about 13.5 miles, and the wilderness area will be on your right.

GPS Coordinates: 36.13993°N, 107.92071°W

Did You Know?
The term "Ah-Shi-Sle-Pah" means "gray salt," likely named because of its eroded badlands, vegetation-less area, and the fact that much of the area looks like a gray rock. The Ah-Shi-Sle-Pah Wilderness boasts truly unique geological formations and fossils. While you are hiking around, it's not uncommon for you to see hoodoos, petrified logs, and stumps.

Journal:

Date(s) Visited:

Weather conditions:

Who you were with:

Nature observations:

Special memories:

Caballo Lake; Sierra County

For camping, hiking, kayaking, boating, canoeing, swimming, and fishing, Caballo Lake State Park is a fantastic place to visit. Located 20 miles downstream from Elephant Butte and featuring the Caballo Mountains as its background, this lake has some incredible scenic views. Not only is the area known for bird watching, but visitors have reported sunrises and sunsets that will take your breath away.

Best time to visit:
The summer will have the warmest temperatures to enjoy the water activities, but it will also be the busiest season.

Pass/Permit/Fees:
There is a $5 fee to enter the park.

Closest city or town: Truth or Consequences, NM

How to get there:
The Caballo State Park is located 16 miles south of Truth or Consequences. You can take the old HWY-187 or get off Exit 59 of I-25.

GPS Coordinates: 32.9257° N, 107.2961° W

Did You Know?
Sierra County is also home to New Mexico's largest body of water, Elephant Butte Lake. Elephant Butte Lake sits on a 40,000-acre park and has opportunities for hiking, camping, and some of New Mexico's best fishing. If you're interested in fishing for record-sized black, white, and striped bass, then this may be the destination for you. If you are only visiting the area for a few days and do not have your own boat, there are several places that will rent out boats for the day.

Journal:

Date(s) Visited:

Weather conditions:

Who you were with:

Nature observations:

Special memories:

Shiprock

Shiprock Peak is a towering volcanic rock formation that summits at 7,178 feet above sea level. At the center of three separate volcanic pressure ridges, this geological feature is truly a sight to be seen. This rock formation is sacred to the Navajo people and is known in the Navajo language as *"Tsé Bit' a'i,"* meaning "rock with wings." Hiking or climbing Shiprock is not allowed because it is sacred ground, but you can still get picturesque views of the structure from a dirt road.

Best time to visit:
You can visit the structure year-round from the paved roads that view the structure.

Pass/Permit/Fees:
No fees are required to view Shiprock.

Closest city or town: Shiprock, NM

How to get there:
The two paved roadways are Indian Service Route 13 and US HWY-491. You can see the peak from 30 to 50 miles away, but the best viewing is west of Farmington, NM on HWY-64 or south of Shiprock on HWY 491.

GPS Coordinates: 36.7856° N, 108.6870° W

Did You Know?
If you want to walk in the footsteps of some of your favorite actors, make sure to visit Shiprock. Shiprock has made several appearances in movies, such as *Transformers* (2007), *John Carter* (2012), *Natural Born Killers* (1994), *The Host* (2013), *The Lone Ranger* (2013), *Jumanji: The Next Level* (2019), and others.

Journal:

Date(s) Visited:

Weather
conditions:

Who you were with:

Nature observations:

Special memories:

Spence Hot Springs

Spence Hot Springs is a small pool that is located in the Santa Fe National Forest. The springs maintain a temperature of 95°F in the springtime, and even though the temperature remains close to human body temperature, the pool will feel heavenly on a chilly spring, fall, or winter day. Visitors can hike an easy trail to the springs. The Spence Hot Springs Trailhead is rated for all skill levels, so every visitor can enjoy the gorgeous scenic views and then soak in the springs.

Best time to visit:
While the busiest season is in the summer, the best time to visit the hot springs is in the fall and winter.

Pass/Permit/Fees:
No passes are required to hike to the hot springs.

Closest city or town: Jemez Springs, NM

How to get there:
The hot springs are located about a quarter of a mile from NM-4. From Jemez Springs, drive north on NM-4 for seven miles. There will be a paved parking lot indicating the location of the springs.

GPS Coordinates: 35.8495° N, 106.6298° W

Did You Know?
Hot springs are heated by geothermal heat from inside the Earth's crust. In areas where volcanos once erupted, the springs are heated by subsurface magma that heats groundwater and produces steam. In areas with no volcanic activity, the temperature of the rocks under the spring will get warmer as they become closer to the Earth's interior (i.e., the deeper the rocks, the warmer they are). This is known as the Geothermal Gradient.

Journal:

Date(s) Visited:

Weather conditions:

Who you were with:

Nature observations:

Special memories:

Taos Gorge/Rio Grande Gorge

The Taos Gorge is an 800-foot-long gorge that has been carved by the Rio Grande. The rock of the gorge is comprised of volcanic basalt and ash, making this gorge an utterly unique sight. Visitors can hike the six-mile-long Rio Grande Gorge Trail that dips into the gorge and covers an impressive 1,309 feet in elevation.

Best time to visit:
The trails and bridge are available to visit year-round. However, the trail has been closed for long-term construction as of January 2021, so make sure to check trail conditions before you go.

Pass/Permit/Fees:
No fees are required to hike the trails or visit the gorge's bridge.

Closest city or town: Taos, NM

How to get there:
To get to the gorge, take US HWY-64 (New Mexico State Road 522) north for 3.5 miles. This will take you to the last four-way intersection in the area. Take a left on US HWY-64 West and drive eight miles. You will arrive at a parking lot.

GPS Coordinates: 36.4762° N, 105.7330° W

Did You Know?
The Gorge Bridge sits 650 feet above the Rio Grande and is the fifth-highest bridge in the United States. Originally called "the bridge to nowhere," the Rio Grande Gorge Bridge was dedicated in 1965 and is currently part of US Route 64. If you can conquer your fear of heights and cross the bridge, you will experience spectacular views of the gorge and the landscape surrounding the Rio Grande.

Journal:

Date(s) Visited:

Weather conditions:

Who you were with:

Nature observations:

Special memories:

Other Places

Place: _____

Date(s) visited:

Weather conditions:

Whom you were with:

Nature observations:

Special memories:

Place: _____

Date(s) visited:

Weather conditions:

Whom you were with:

Nature observations:

Special memories:

Place: _____

Date(s) visited:

Weather conditions:

Whom you were with:

Nature observations:

Special memories:

Place: _____

Date(s) visited:

Weather conditions:

Whom you were with:

Nature observations:

Special memories:

Place: _____

Date(s) visited:

Weather conditions:

Whom you were with:

Nature observations:

Special memories:

Place: _____

Date(s) visited:

Weather conditions:

Whom you were with:

Nature observations:

Special memories:

Place: _____

Date(s) visited:

Weather conditions:

Whom you were with:

Nature observations:

Special memories:

Place: _____

Date(s) visited:

Weather conditions:

Whom you were with:

Nature observations:

Special memories:

Place: _____

Date(s) visited:

Weather conditions:

Whom you were with:

Nature observations:

Special memories:

Place: _____

Date(s) visited:

Weather conditions:

Whom you were with:

Nature observations:

Special memories:

Credit the Incredible Photographers:

124

North Fork Casa Falls
https://search.creativecommons.org/photos/25a34a6a-bc6d-4b3c-b6ed-7d8feec6604b
"Dodie under one of the North Fork's falls" by Eric Gropp is licensed with CC BY 2.0. To view a copy of this license, visit https://creativecommons.org/licenses/by/2.0/

Upper Frijoles Falls
https://search.creativecommons.org/photos/2929550e-4162-47ef-9df9-b4c0470f2955
"Bandelier National Monument" by Crown Star Images is licensed with CC BY 2.0. To view a copy of this license, visit https://creativecommons.org/licenses/by/2.0/

Fillmore Waterfall New Mexico
https://search.creativecommons.org/photos/7067fb0e-6fa3-46b3-b823-f95139a3aefc
"Fillmore Canyon Waterfall" by Frank Carey is licensed with CC BY-NC-SA 2.0. To view a copy of this license, visit https://creativecommons.org/licenses/by-nc-sa/2.0/

Holden Prong Cascades
https://search.creativecommons.org/photos/aa8238df-9125-4432-adf0-89bc0034de9c
"W. Fk of Mogollon crk, Jeanie's waterfall, Gila National Forest" by Gila National Forest Photography is licensed with CC BY-SA 2.0. To view a copy of this license, visit https://creativecommons.org/licenses/by-sa/2.0/

Heron Lake; Rio Arriba County
https://search.creativecommons.org/photos/1f0063cd-9bec-40d7-95b7-8acd834e04a7
"Heron Lake" by Karsun Designs Photography is licensed with CC BY 2.0. To view a copy of this license, visit https://creativecommons.org/licenses/by/2.0/

Turquoise Trail
https://search.creativecommons.org/photos/3d3bf991-1e4d-4f44-b483-8b5ebc0e7a72
"Somewhere along the Turquoise Trail" by rgallant_photography is licensed with CC BY 2.0. To view a copy of this license, visit https://creativecommons.org/licenses/by/2.0/

Camel Rock
https://search.creativecommons.org/photos/43584655-0e59-417b-9964-b9a6de0cbe15
"Camel Rock at Sunset" by Kevin Eddy is licensed with CC BY-NC-ND 2.0. To view a copy of this license, visit https://creativecommons.org/licenses/by-nc-nd/2.0/

Bosque del Apache National Wildlife Refuge
https://search.creativecommons.org/photos/f19f9fb4-619d-461c-b8c8-7c9346ba8177
"Festival of the Cranes at Bosque del Apache National WIldlife Refuge 2016" by U.S. Fish & Wildlife Service Southwest Region is marked under CC PDM 1.0. To view the terms, visit https://creativecommons.org/publicdomain/mark/1.0/

Brazos Cliffs
https://search.creativecommons.org/photos/c78c391d-e9cd-4226-a5d8-d6b4e12ed1ce
"Brazos Cliffs and Valley, New Mexico" by ToGa Wanderings is licensed with CC BY 2.0. To view a copy of this license, visit https://creativecommons.org/licenses/by/2.0/

Capulin Volcano National Monument
https://search.creativecommons.org/photos/a6daac6a-901a-444d-b0d7-f451987ad1df
"Capulin Volcano National Monument" by jaygannett is licensed with CC BY-SA 2.0. To view a copy of this license, visit https://creativecommons.org/licenses/by-sa/2.0/

Chaco Canyon
https://search.creativecommons.org/photos/5e66e6ea-2758-4696-a77e-c614756de78e

Made in the USA
Coppell, TX
15 June 2022

78864226R00070